Inside the Paris Olympics 2024

Your Comprehensive Guide to the Paris Olympic Games

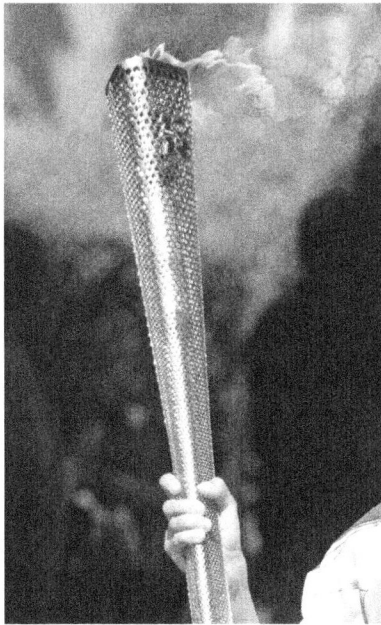

By

Martina Lecazite

Table of Contents

1. Introduction to the Olympic Games

1.1. History and Origins:

The Olympic Games have their roots deeply embedded in ancient Greek civilization, where they were inaugurated in 776 BCE in Olympia, a sacred sanctuary dedicated to Zeus, the king of the Greek gods. These ancient competitions encompassed a variety of athletic contests, including running, wrestling, chariot racing, and the pentathlon.

Originating as a celebration of physical prowess and cultural exchange, the ancient Olympics held profound significance in Greek society, serving as a symbol of unity among city-states and a platform for fostering camaraderie and competition among athletes.

1.2. Significance of the Olympic Games:

The Olympic Games hold a unique place in global culture, symbolizing ideals of peace, solidarity, and sportsmanship. They transcend geographical, cultural, and political boundaries, bringing together nations in the pursuit of excellence and mutual respect.

Beyond their athletic spectacle, the Games serve as a beacon of hope and inspiration, promoting values of determination, perseverance, and fair play. They provide a stage for athletes to showcase their talents and inspire others, while also fostering dialogue and understanding among diverse cultures.

1.3. Evolution of the Modern Olympics:

Pierre de Coubertin's vision in 1896 revived the ancient Olympic spirit, leading to the establishment of the modern Olympic Games in Athens, Greece. From its humble beginnings, the modern Olympics have grown into a global phenomenon, expanding to include a diverse array of sports and disciplines.

Embracing innovation and progress, the Games have adapted to changing times, incorporating new technologies and evolving formats while upholding their core principles of excellence and unity. Today, the Olympics stand as a testament to human achievement and cooperation, inspiring generations to pursue their dreams and contribute to a brighter future for all.

2. The Host City: Paris 2024

2.1. Overview of Paris as the Host City:

Paris, the enchanting capital of France, stands proudly as the chosen host for the 2024 Olympic Games. Revered for its timeless allure, cultural richness, and architectural splendor, Paris promises a breathtaking backdrop for this global event. As one of the world's most beloved destinations, the city captivates with its historic landmarks, vibrant atmosphere, and unmatched elegance.

The honor of hosting the Olympics allows Paris to exhibit its diverse cultural tapestry, forward-thinking ethos, and dedication to sustainability on a world stage. The city's iconic monuments, such as the majestic Eiffel Tower, illustrious Louvre Museum, and majestic Notre-Dame Cathedral, will serve as enduring symbols of the Games, adding a touch of magic and prestige to the occasion.

2.2. Selection Process for Host City:

Paris's designation as the host city for the 2024 Olympics followed a rigorous selection process overseen by the International Olympic Committee (IOC). Competing against other prominent candidates, Paris presented a compelling bid showcasing its vision, capabilities, and commitment to hosting a remarkable Games.

The city's successful bid was bolstered by its extensive infrastructure, proven track record in hosting major events, and unwavering public enthusiasm. Paris's emphasis on sustainability, legacy planning, and inclusivity resonated strongly with the IOC, cementing its status as the ideal host city.

2.3. Infrastructure and Venues:

Paris boasts a robust infrastructure network encompassing modern transportation systems, diverse accommodations, and world-class venues. The city's comprehensive public transit system, including metro lines, buses, and trains, ensures seamless mobility for athletes, officials, and spectators alike.

In preparation for the 2024 Olympics, Paris will optimize its existing infrastructure while implementing strategic upgrades to meet the demands of the Games. Iconic venues such as the Stade de France, Roland Garros Stadium, and Paris Expo Porte de Versailles will serve as prestigious settings for various sporting events, offering top-tier facilities and immersive spectator experiences.

Furthermore, Paris is committed to embracing innovative and sustainable practices in venue design and construction, aligning with the IOC's vision of environmental stewardship and lasting legacies. These meticulously planned venues will not only showcase athletic excellence during the Games but also leave an indelible mark on the city, enriching its cultural landscape and enhancing its future prosperity.

3. Paris 2024 Olympic Games: Overview

3.1. Dates and Duration:

The Paris 2024 Olympic Games are scheduled to take place from July 26th to August 11th, 2024. This period spans over two weeks, during which various sporting events and competitions will be held across multiple venues in and around Paris, France.

3.2. Participating Countries:

The Paris 2024 Olympics are expected to feature participation from a diverse array of countries around the world. Athletes representing their respective nations will converge in Paris to compete in various sports and disciplines. The Olympic Games traditionally attract participants from over 200 countries, making it a truly global event that celebrates athletic prowess and international camaraderie.

3.3. Key Events and Competitions:

Paris 2024 will showcase a wide range of sporting events and competitions, encompassing both traditional Olympic sports and newly introduced disciplines. Some of the key events to watch out for include:

1. **Athletics (Track and Field):** Featuring sprinting, long-distance running, jumping, throwing, and combined events such as the decathlon and heptathlon.

2. **Swimming and Aquatics:** Including swimming, diving, synchronized swimming, and water polo competitions held in state-of-the-art aquatic centers.

3. **Gymnastics:** Showcasing artistic gymnastics, rhythmic gymnastics, and trampoline events, highlighting agility, strength, and grace.

4. **Team Sports:** Such as basketball, football (soccer), volleyball, handball, and rugby sevens, where national teams compete for Olympic glory.

5. **Cycling:** Featuring road cycling, track cycling, mountain biking, and BMX events held in various scenic locations around Paris.

6. **Equestrian Sports:** Including dressage, show jumping, and eventing, where horse and rider combinations demonstrate precision and skill.

7. **Sailing:** Held at designated sailing venues, showcasing competition across various classes and disciplines on the water.

8. **Fencing:** Showcasing the art of swordsmanship and skillful duels between competitors in various fencing disciplines.

9. **Weightlifting:** Demonstrating feats of strength and technique as athletes compete to lift the heaviest weights in different weight categories.

10. **New Sports and Disciplines:** Paris 2024 will also introduce new sports and disciplines, aligning with the Olympic Agenda 2020+5 goals to innovate and appeal to younger audiences. These may include skateboarding, surfing, sport climbing, and additional events aimed at enhancing the Olympic experience for participants and spectators alike.

These key events and competitions, among many others, will captivate audiences worldwide as athletes strive for excellence and national pride on the grand stage of the Paris 2024 Olympic Games.

4. Olympic Sports and Disciplines:

4.1. Summer Olympic Sports:

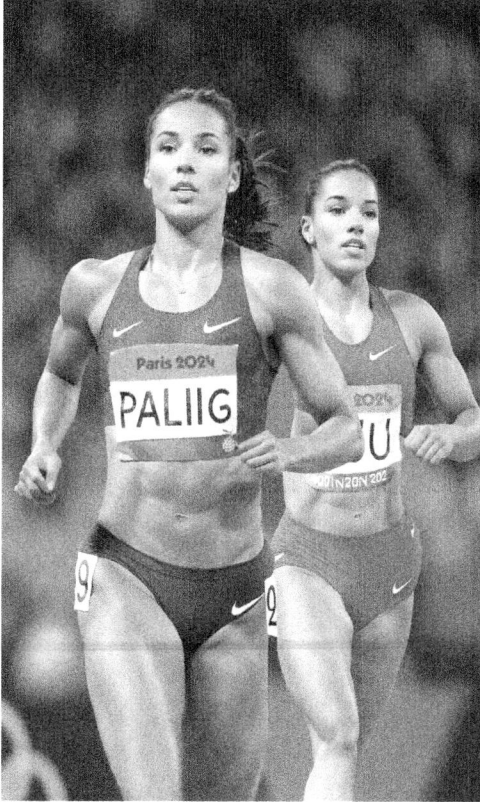

The Summer Olympic Games host a rich tapestry of sports, showcasing the pinnacle of athleticism, endurance, and skill. These sports encompass a wide array of disciplines, offering a global stage for athletes to compete at the highest level. Among the enduring staples of the Summer Olympics are:

- Athletics (Track and Field)

- Swimming

- Gymnastics

- Cycling (Road, Track, Mountain Bike, BMX)

- Tennis

- Basketball

- Football (Soccer)

- Volleyball (Beach and Indoor)

- Wrestling

- Boxing

- Sailing

- Rowing

- Equestrian (Dressage, Eventing, Jumping)

- Archery

- Shooting

- Fencing

- Judo

- Taekwondo

- Table Tennis

- Badminton

- Triathlon

- Weightlifting

- Canoeing and Kayaking (Sprint, Slalom)

These disciplines offer a blend of individual and team competitions, providing a platform for athletes worldwide to showcase their talents and vie for Olympic glory.

4.2. New Sports and Disciplines in Paris 2024:

The Paris 2024 Olympic Games herald the arrival of new sports and disciplines to the Olympic stage, reflecting evolving trends and interests in the sporting landscape. These additions seek to broaden the Olympics' appeal and engage fresh audiences. While specific sports and disciplines may vary, prospective inclusions could comprise:

- Surfing

- Skateboarding

- Sport Climbing

- Breakdancing (Breaking)

- Mixed Team Events (e.g., Mixed Gender Relays)

- Additional disciplines within existing sports (e.g., new events in athletics, swimming, or cycling)

These innovations align with the International Olympic Committee's (IOC) drive to modernize and invigorate the Olympic program, ensuring its resonance with contemporary sporting culture.

4.3. Paralympic Sports:

The Paralympic Games serve as a stage for extraordinary feats by athletes with physical disabilities, fostering inclusivity, diversity, and excellence in sports. Paralympic sports are categorized based on athletes' impairments, ensuring equitable competition and opportunities for all participants. Among the Paralympic sports featured in the Summer Paralympic Games are:

- Athletics

- Swimming

- Wheelchair Basketball

- Wheelchair Rugby

- Wheelchair Tennis

- Para-Cycling (Road, Track)

- Sitting Volleyball

- Para-Rowing

- Goalball

- Boccia

- Wheelchair Fencing

- Para-Taekwondo

- Para-Archery

- Powerlifting

- Para-Canoeing

- Wheelchair Racing

These sports epitomize determination, resilience, and sportsmanship, inspiring audiences worldwide and challenging perceptions of disability and sports. The Paralympic Games celebrate the remarkable abilities of para-athletes and promote inclusivity and accessibility in sports across all levels.

5. Paris 2024 Olympic Legacy

5.1. Socio-Economic Impact:

The hosting of the Olympic Games in Paris in 2024 is poised to generate a substantial socio-economic impact on both the city and the broader French economy. The influx of visitors, athletes, and media coverage during the event is projected to stimulate economic growth through increased spending across various sectors, including hospitality, transportation, retail, and entertainment.

The investment in infrastructure required for the Games, such as the construction and renovation of stadiums, transportation networks, and urban facilities, will not only support the successful execution of the event but also leave a lasting legacy for Parisians. These infrastructure developments are expected to enhance the city's attractiveness, improve accessibility, and catalyze urban regeneration in underdeveloped areas.

Moreover, the creation of job opportunities in sectors like construction, tourism, and event management will contribute to reducing unemployment rates and fostering economic development in the region. Additionally, the legacy of improved infrastructure and facilities can attract future investments and promote sustainable growth beyond the Olympic Games.

5.2. Sustainability Initiatives:

Paris 2024 is committed to delivering the most sustainable Olympic Games to date, aligning with the International Olympic Committee's sustainability agenda. The organizers are implementing a range of initiatives to minimize the environmental impact of the Games and promote sustainable practices across all facets of the event.

Efforts to reduce carbon emissions include prioritizing low-emission transportation options, such as public transit, cycling, and walking, and promoting energy-efficient technologies in venue construction and operations. Waste reduction strategies, such as recycling programs and minimizing single-use plastics, aim to minimize the environmental footprint of the Games.

Furthermore, Paris 2024 is leveraging the platform of the Olympics to raise awareness about environmental issues and inspire action towards a more sustainable future. Educational programs, community engagement initiatives, and sustainability-themed events will empower citizens and visitors to adopt eco-friendly behaviors and contribute to global conservation efforts.

5.3. Cultural and Social Implications:

Beyond the sporting spectacle, Paris 2024 presents an opportunity to showcase the rich cultural heritage and diversity of France to a global audience. Cultural programs, exhibitions, and artistic performances will celebrate the country's artistic traditions, gastronomy, and cultural innovations, fostering cross-cultural exchange and appreciation.

The Games will also serve as a platform for promoting inclusivity and diversity, with a focus on gender equality, accessibility, and social inclusion. Initiatives to empower marginalized communities, promote social cohesion, and celebrate the achievements of athletes from diverse backgrounds will underscore the Olympic values of solidarity and respect.

Moreover, Paris 2024 aims to inspire the next generation of athletes and leaders through sports participation programs, educational initiatives, and youth engagement activities. By showcasing the extraordinary feats of athletes and promoting the values of perseverance, teamwork, and fair play, the Games will leave a lasting legacy of inspiration and empowerment for future generations.

6. Athletes of Paris 2024

6.1. Profiles of Key Athletes:

1. **Simone Biles (United States**) - Widely regarded as one of the greatest gymnasts of all time, Biles is expected to showcase her incredible talent and athleticism in Paris 2024. With multiple Olympic gold medals under her belt, including the individual all-around title, Biles continues to push the boundaries of the sport with her unmatched skills.

2. **Usain Bolt (Jamaica)** - Although retired from professional athletics, Bolt remains a towering figure in the world of sports. As the fastest man in history, his legacy looms large over the track and field events of Paris 2024. Bolt's electrifying performances and charismatic personality have made him an icon of the Olympic Games.

3. **Yusra Mardini (Refugee Olympic Team)** - Mardini captured the world's attention with her remarkable journey from Syrian refugee to Olympic swimmer. Competing under the Refugee Olympic Team banner, her story symbolizes the resilience and determination of athletes overcoming adversity.

6.2. Training and Preparation:

1. **Intensive Training Camps:** Athletes from around the globe dedicate countless hours to rigorous training regimes in preparation for the Olympic Games. From grueling gym sessions to meticulously planned practice drills, every aspect of their training is geared towards peak performance on the world stage.

2. **Specialized Coaching:** Many athletes enlist the expertise of top coaches and trainers to fine-tune their skills and develop winning strategies. These coaches provide invaluable guidance, helping athletes optimize their physical and mental capabilities for the demands of elite competition.

3. **Nutrition and Recovery:** Proper nutrition and rest are essential components of an athlete's training regimen. Nutritionists work closely with athletes to develop customized meal plans that fuel their performance and support optimal recovery. Techniques such as ice baths, massage therapy, and physiotherapy are also employed to keep athletes in peak condition.

6.3. Inspirational Stories:

1. **Overcoming Adversity:** The journey to the Olympics is often fraught with challenges and setbacks. Many athletes have overcome

adversity, whether it be injury, illness, or personal hardship, to achieve their Olympic dreams. Their stories of resilience and perseverance inspire people around the world to never give up on their goals.

2. **Unity and Friendship:** The Olympic Games serve as a platform for athletes from diverse backgrounds to come together in the spirit of sportsmanship and camaraderie. Inspirational stories abound of athletes forming deep bonds with competitors from rival nations, demonstrating the unifying power of sport to transcend cultural and political divides.

3. **Making History:** Every Olympic Games produces moments of triumph and glory that capture the imagination of millions. From record-breaking performances to underdog victories, these historic achievements inspire future generations of athletes to aim for greatness. The pursuit of excellence, both on and off the field of play, is a hallmark of the Olympic spirit.

7. Technology and Innovation in Paris 2024

7.1. Role of Technology in Paris 2024:

- **Data Analytics and Performance Tracking:** Advanced technologies will monitor athletes' performance, employing wearable sensors, video analysis software, and biometric monitoring systems to provide real-time feedback to coaches and athletes.

- **Venue Management Systems:** Integrated technology will streamline venue operations, managing crowd flow, security, and logistics efficiently to ensure a seamless experience for athletes, spectators, and staff.

- **Sustainability Initiatives:** Paris 2024 will implement innovative technology for energy conservation, waste management, and eco-friendly transportation, utilizing smart buildings, renewable energy sources, and waste reduction strategies to promote environmental sustainability.

7.2. Advancements in Sports Equipment:

- **Materials Science:** Cutting-edge materials and manufacturing techniques will enhance sports equipment, making it lighter, more durable, and better suited to athletes' needs. From carbon fiber bicycles to aerodynamic swimsuits, advancements in materials science will offer athletes a competitive advantage.

- **Biomechanics and Design:** Sports equipment will be optimized through biomechanical analysis and ergonomic design, with customized footwear, ergonomic grips, and aerodynamic helmets tailored to individual athletes' biomechanics and performance objectives.

- **Innovations in Safety:** Safety will be prioritized in sports equipment design, with features such as impact-absorbing padding, concussion-prevention technologies, and improved protective gear contributing to athletes' well-being and injury prevention.

7.3. 3. Broadcast and Viewing Experience:

- **Immersive Viewing Technologies:** Paris 2024 will provide immersive experiences through virtual reality (VR), augmented reality (AR), and 360-degree video technology, allowing spectators to engage with the Games in interactive ways.

- **Enhanced Coverage and Accessibility:** Broadcasting technologies will ensure comprehensive coverage of the Olympic Games, with multiple channels, streaming platforms, and accessibility features catering to diverse audiences worldwide.

- **Social Media Integration:** Social media platforms will play a central role in the broadcast experience, offering live updates, behind-the-scenes content, and interactive features to enhance audience engagement and foster a sense of global community.

8. Spectator Experience

8.1. Ticketing Information:

- Overview: The ticketing process for the Paris 2024 Olympic Games aims to provide fair access to spectators from around the world.

- Ticket Categories: Tickets will be available for various sports and events, including opening and closing ceremonies, athletics, swimming, gymnastics, and more.

- Pricing: Ticket prices will vary depending on the event, seat location, and demand.

- Availability: Tickets can be purchased online through the official Paris 2024 website, authorized ticket resellers, or designated ticketing centers.

- Accessibility: Special provisions will be made for accessible seating and accommodations for individuals with disabilities.

8.2. Fan Zones and Activities:

- Overview: Paris 2024 will feature vibrant fan zones and activities throughout the city to enhance the spectator experience.

- Locations: Fan zones will be strategically located in prominent areas, including near competition venues, city centers, and iconic landmarks.

- Entertainment: Spectators can enjoy live music, cultural performances, interactive exhibits, and food and beverage offerings.

- Meet-and-Greets: Opportunities to meet athletes, participate in autograph sessions, and engage in sports-related activities will be available.

- Family-Friendly: Family-friendly zones with activities for children and families will cater to a diverse range of spectators.

8.3. Travel and Accommodation Tips:

- Transportation: Spectators are advised to plan their transportation in advance, utilizing public transportation options such as buses, trains, and metros. Special event shuttles may also be available.

- Accommodation: Booking accommodations well in advance is recommended due to high demand during the Olympic Games. Options include hotels, hostels, Airbnb rentals, and accommodations within designated Olympic villages.

- Location Considerations: Choose accommodations that offer convenient access to competition venues, fan zones, and key attractions.

- Security and Safety: Familiarize yourself with safety protocols and emergency procedures. Be vigilant and mindful of your belongings in crowded areas.

- Cultural Exploration: Take advantage of your time in Paris to explore the city's rich cultural heritage, iconic landmarks, and culinary delights outside of Olympic events.

By considering these details, spectators can ensure a memorable and enjoyable experience at the Paris 2024 Olympic Games.

9. Legacy Beyond the Games:

9.1. Urban Development Projects:

- Urban regeneration and infrastructure improvements often accompany the hosting of the Olympic Games. In the case of Paris 2024, significant investments are made in enhancing transportation networks, building new sports facilities, and revitalizing public spaces.

- The development of Olympic-related infrastructure such as stadiums, athlete villages, and transportation systems leaves a lasting legacy that benefits the host city long after the Games have concluded.

- These projects aim to improve the quality of life for residents, stimulate economic growth, and enhance the city's attractiveness to visitors and investors.

9.2. Community Engagement Initiatives:

- The legacy of the Olympic Games extends to fostering community engagement and social inclusion. Paris 2024 organizers implement various programs and initiatives to involve local communities, promote diversity, and encourage participation in sports and cultural activities.

- Community engagement initiatives may include sports clinics, cultural events, educational programs, and volunteer opportunities. These initiatives aim to empower residents, especially youth, and promote values such as teamwork, respect, and fair play.

- By engaging with diverse communities and stakeholders, the Olympic Games leave a positive social legacy that strengthens community bonds and promotes social cohesion.

9.3. Long-Term Impact on Sports Culture:

- Hosting the Olympic Games can have a profound and lasting impact on the sports culture of the host city and country. Paris 2024 aims to inspire a new generation of athletes and enthusiasts, promoting active lifestyles and sports participation.

- The Games provide opportunities to showcase a wide range of sports and disciplines, raising awareness and interest in less mainstream sports. This exposure can lead to increased participation and investment in grassroots sports programs.

- Furthermore, the Olympic legacy includes the development of high-performance training facilities, coaching programs, and sports academies, nurturing talent and excellence in various sports disciplines.

- Beyond elite competition, the Olympic legacy encourages a culture of sportsmanship, fair play, and inclusivity, shaping attitudes and behaviors towards sports and physical activity in the host community for years to come.

10. Cultural Events and Entertainment

10.1. Cultural Festivals and Events during the Olympics:

Paris, renowned for its rich cultural heritage, will host a myriad of festivals and events during the 2024 Olympics, offering visitors a chance to immerse themselves in the city's vibrant atmosphere. Some of the notable cultural events include:

1. **Festival d'Avignon Offshoot:** Experience a taste of the famed Festival d'Avignon, one of the world's most prestigious theater festivals, with special performances and showcases brought to Paris during the Olympics.

2. **Paris Jazz Festival:** Jazz enthusiasts will delight in the Paris Jazz Festival, featuring a lineup of international and local artists performing in scenic outdoor venues across the city.

3. **Montmartre Wine Festival:** Held in the picturesque Montmartre district, this annual festival celebrates the rich tradition of winemaking in Paris with wine tastings, live music, and cultural exhibitions.

4. **Fête de la Musique:** Join the city-wide celebration of music on June 21st, as Paris comes alive with free concerts and performances in streets, squares, and parks, showcasing diverse musical genres and talents.

5. **Fashion Week Events:** Paris Fashion Week coinciding with the Olympics promises a flurry of fashion shows, exhibitions, and parties, showcasing the latest trends and designs from top fashion houses and emerging designers.

10.2.   Must-Visit Attractions in Paris:

While in Paris for the Olympics, visitors have an abundance of iconic attractions to explore, each offering a unique glimpse into the city's history and culture. Some must-visit attractions include:

1. **Eiffel Tower:** No visit to Paris is complete without ascending the iconic Eiffel Tower for panoramic views of the cityscape and the Seine River below.

2. **Louvre Museum:** Discover world-famous masterpieces at the Louvre Museum, including the Mona Lisa, Venus de Milo, and Winged Victory of Samothrace, housed within the historic Louvre Palace.

3. **Notre-Dame Cathedral:** Despite the tragic fire in 2019, Notre-Dame Cathedral remains a symbol of Parisian Gothic architecture, offering visitors a chance to admire its stunning façade and interior.

4. **Montmartre:** Wander through the charming streets of Montmartre, home to the iconic Sacré-Cœur Basilica, bustling artist squares, and picturesque cafés immortalized by artists like Picasso and Van Gogh.

5. **Champs-Élysées:** Stroll down the famous Champs-Élysées boulevard, lined with luxury boutiques, theaters, and cafés, culminating at the majestic Arc de Triomphe.

10.3.   Entertainment Options for Visitors:

Paris offers a plethora of entertainment options to suit every taste and interest, ensuring visitors have a memorable experience beyond the Olympic events. Here are some recommendations:

1. **Theater and Cabaret Shows:** Catch a captivating theater production or indulge in an evening of cabaret at renowned venues like the Moulin Rouge or the Opéra Garnier.

2. **Cruise on the Seine:** Embark on a scenic cruise along the Seine River, admiring Paris's iconic landmarks illuminated against the night sky while enjoying onboard entertainment and dining.

3. **Concerts and Performances:** Attend a classical concert at the Opéra Bastille, a ballet performance at the Palais Garnier, or a contemporary music gig at one of Paris's many live music venues.

4. **Nightlife in Le Marais:** Experience Paris's vibrant nightlife scene in the trendy Le Marais district, known for its eclectic mix of bars, clubs, and LGBTQ+ venues, offering something for everyone.

5. **Outdoor Activities:** Take advantage of Paris's beautiful parks and gardens for leisurely picnics, jogging, or simply soaking in the atmosphere amidst lush greenery and scenic views.

With its rich cultural tapestry and diverse entertainment offerings, Paris promises an unforgettable experience for visitors attending the 2024 Olympics, ensuring they leave with cherished memories of their time in the City of Light.

11. Dining and Cuisine in Paris

Paris is renowned worldwide for its exquisite culinary scene, offering a tantalizing array of flavors and dishes that cater to every palate. From quaint bistros to Michelin-starred restaurants, the city's dining options promise a gastronomic adventure like no other. Here's a detailed look at dining and cuisine in Paris:

11.1.   Culinary Delights of Paris:

Parisian cuisine is celebrated for its elegance, sophistication, and emphasis on fresh, high-quality ingredients. The city's culinary heritage is deeply rooted in traditional French cooking techniques, but it also embraces global influences, resulting in a diverse and vibrant food culture.

11.2.   Recommended Restaurants and Eateries:

1. **Le Jules Verne:** Situated on the second floor of the Eiffel Tower, Le Jules Verne offers breathtaking views of Paris alongside exquisite French cuisine curated by renowned chef Alain Ducasse.

2. **L'Astrance:** This three-Michelin-starred restaurant is a culinary gem, known for its innovative and artistic approach to French gastronomy. Chef Pascal Barbot's tasting menu showcases the finest seasonal ingredients with flair.

3. **Buvette:** For a more relaxed dining experience, head to Buvette, a cozy bistro in the vibrant Pigalle neighborhood. Enjoy an eclectic menu featuring French-inspired small plates, charcuterie, and an impressive selection of wines.

4. **Les Deux Magots:** Steeped in history, Les Deux Magots is a legendary café in the heart of Saint-Germain-des-Prés. Frequented by writers, artists, and intellectuals, this iconic establishment offers classic French fare in an iconic setting.

5. **Marché des Enfants Rouges:** Paris' oldest covered market, Marché des Enfants Rouges, is a culinary treasure trove where visitors can sample a diverse range of cuisines, from Moroccan tagines to Japanese bento boxes.

11.3.   Specialties and Local Dishes to Try:

1. **Croissant:** Start your day like a true Parisian with a buttery, flaky croissant from one of the city's artisanal bakeries. Pair it with a café au lait for the quintessential French breakfast experience.

2. **Coq au Vin:** This classic French dish features tender chicken braised in red wine with mushrooms, onions, and bacon. Served with creamy mashed potatoes or crusty baguette, it's a hearty and comforting meal.

3. **Boeuf Bourguignon:** Another beloved French staple, boeuf bourguignon is a rich and flavorful beef stew simmered in red wine with onions, carrots, and aromatic herbs. It's the epitome of French comfort food.

4. **Macarons:** Indulge your sweet tooth with Paris' famous macarons – delicate almond meringue cookies filled with luscious ganache or buttercream. Sample an array of flavors, from classic raspberry to exotic passion fruit.

5. **Escargots:** For the adventurous foodie, escargots (snails) are a quintessential French delicacy. Served in garlic butter or parsley sauce, they're surprisingly delicious and pair well with crusty bread and a glass of white wine.

In Paris, dining isn't just about nourishment – it's a sensory experience that celebrates the art of food and conviviality. Whether you're savoring a decadent meal at a Michelin-starred restaurant or enjoying a simple baguette sandwich by the Seine, every bite tells a story of culinary excellence and cultural richness. Bon appétit!

12. Safety and Security

12.1. Safety Measures Implemented for the Olympics:

- **Security Personnel:** The Paris 2024 Olympics will deploy a significant number of security personnel, including police officers, security guards, and trained volunteers, to ensure the safety of participants and spectators alike.

- **Surveillance Systems:** State-of-the-art surveillance systems, including CCTV cameras and monitoring stations, will be strategically placed throughout the Olympic venues and key areas of Paris to monitor activities and respond swiftly to any security threats.

- **Bag Checks and Screening:** Enhanced security measures, such as bag checks and screenings, will be conducted at all entry points to the Olympic venues to prevent unauthorized items from entering and to ensure the safety of everyone attending the events.

- **Collaboration with International Agencies:** The organizers of the Paris 2024 Olympics will collaborate closely with international security agencies and organizations to exchange intelligence, assess potential risks, and implement coordinated security measures to safeguard the games.

- **Cybersecurity Measures:** Robust cybersecurity measures will be in place to protect critical infrastructure, information systems, and digital platforms associated with the Olympics from cyber threats and attacks.

12.2. Emergency Contacts and Protocols:

- **Emergency Services:** In case of any emergencies, including medical emergencies, accidents, or security incidents, attendees can contact the local emergency services by dialing the universal emergency number in France, which is 112.

- **Olympic Hotline:** The Paris 2024 Olympics will establish a dedicated hotline for reporting emergencies, suspicious activities, or security concerns related to the games. This hotline will be staffed by trained personnel who can provide assistance and coordinate responses as necessary.

- **Medical Facilities:** Medical facilities and first aid stations will be available at all Olympic venues to provide immediate medical assistance to athletes, spectators, and staff in case of injuries, illnesses, or medical emergencies.

12.3.   Tips for Staying Safe in Paris During the Games:

- **Stay Informed:** Stay informed about the latest safety and security updates, including any travel advisories or alerts issued by the local authorities or Olympic organizers. Follow official channels and announcements for accurate information.

- **Be Vigilant:** always Remain vigilant and aware of your surroundings, especially in crowded areas and tourist hotspots. Report any suspicious activities or unattended items to the authorities immediately.

- **Follow Instructions:** Follow the instructions of security personnel and volunteers at the Olympic venues. Cooperate with security checks and screenings to ensure a smooth and secure experience for everyone.

- **Travel Safely:** Use authorized transportation options and designated routes when traveling to and from the Olympic venues. Avoid unauthorized taxis or unlicensed transportation services to minimize the risk of scams or security incidents.

- **Secure Your Belongings:** Keep your belongings always secure, especially in crowded areas and public transportation. Use lockers or secure storage facilities if available to prevent theft or loss of valuables.

- **Stay Connected:** Stay connected with your companions and plan meeting points in case you get separated during the events. Have a communication plan in place to stay in touch in case of emergencies.

By following these safety measures and guidelines, attendees can enjoy the Paris 2024 Olympics with peace of mind, knowing that their safety and security are top priorities for the organizers and authorities.

13. Conclusion: Embracing the Essence of the Olympic Games

13.1.   Reflections on Paris 2024:

Paris 2024 will forever stand as a testament to the enduring spirit of the Olympic Games. As the final cheers fade and the Olympic flame dims, we are left with indelible memories of triumph, unity, and inspiration. The Games showcased the best of humanity, with athletes from every corner of the globe converging in Paris to compete, connect, and celebrate the values of sportsmanship and excellence. Against the backdrop of Paris's iconic landmarks and vibrant culture, the world witnessed unforgettable moments that will echo through history.

Paris 2024 also marked a significant milestone in Olympic history, with its unwavering commitment to sustainability, innovation, and inclusivity. By prioritizing environmentally friendly practices, embracing cutting-edge technology, and championing diversity, Paris set a new standard for future host cities to follow. The legacy of Paris 2024 extends far beyond the sporting arena, leaving a lasting impact on communities, economies, and the global perception of the Olympic movement.

13.2. Looking Ahead to Future Olympic Games:

As Paris bids farewell to the Olympic stage, the world eagerly anticipates the dawn of a new era in Olympic history. With each passing Games, we are reminded of the power of sport to unite, inspire, and transform lives. The future of the Olympic movement holds boundless potential, fueled by the collective efforts of host cities, athletes, and stakeholders to innovate, and evolve.

Moving forward, we must embrace the opportunities and challenges that lie ahead with optimism and determination. By harnessing the spirit of Olympism and embracing principles of sustainability, inclusivity, and excellence, we can ensure that future Olympic Games continue to captivate the hearts and minds of people around the world. Together, let us write the next chapter in the storied legacy of the Olympic Games, guided by the timeless values of friendship, respect, and fair play.

Printed in Great Britain
by Amazon